Madonna, the Piglet Who Grew Up

By Owen McShane

Illustrated by Francis Phillipps

Dominie Press, Inc.

Publisher: Raymond Yuen
Project Editor: John S. F. Graham
Editor: Bob Rowland
Designer: Greg DiGenti
Illustrator: Francis Phillipps

Published by:

‰ Dominie Press, Inc.

1949 Kellogg Avenue
Carlsbad, California 92008 USA

www.dominie.com

1-800-232-4570

Paperback ISBN 0-7685-1815-6
Printed in Singapore by PH Productions Pte Ltd
1 2 3 4 5 6 PH 05 04 03

Table of Contents

Chapter One
A Little Black Piglet....................................5

Chapter Two
Somewhat Bigger...8

Chapter Three
Disgruntled...12

Chapter Four
The Pig Tamer...17

Chapter Five
Twenty-Two Meals a Day!.....................26

Chapter One
A Little Black Piglet

Madonna was a little black piglet.
She lived with the Forester family near
the beach.

Madonna had her own yard and lived
on household scraps. She had small,
bright eyes and a curly tail, and she

"talked" a lot, snuffling and grunting her days away.

Madonna soon became a favorite pet. The neighbors were surprised to see Madonna, the Foresters, and their dog, Blue, walking down the path on their daily visit to the beach.

Blue would bark happily as he ran around the group in big circles, as if to show that Madonna's hoofs were running hard just to keep up. Madonna's tiny curly tail wagged and bounced. She was perfectly happy trotting along. She left the "showing off" to the dog.

Madonna was a lucky pig. She was living with a loving family, and she was fussed over like a favorite pet dog.

Just like a friendly dog in the countryside, Madonna soon began to visit the neighbors.

Chapter Two
Somewhat Bigger

Linda was an artist who lived near the Foresters. One morning, as Linda settled down to work, she heard a friendly grunt and snuffle at the door.

She opened the door, and there stood Madonna, a small piglet, pointing her snout at Linda's hand, then at the floor, and then back at her hand. Madonna's sign language was clear—she wanted a snack.

Linda was charmed by this well-mannered, friendly piglet at her doorstep.

She gave Madonna a potato. Madonna downed the potato in just a few seconds. She looked up to see if there was more to come. When she decided there wasn't, she wandered off.

Linda was so impressed with this sweet little piglet that she decided to make some sketches of her.

The next week, Linda heard that same snuffle again, and a solid thump on the door. She opened the door, and there was Madonna, looking as eager as ever.

Linda noticed, with some unease, that Madonna had gotten somewhat bigger.

She gave the piglet another potato, which disappeared in a gulp.

Madonna showed no signs of leaving after her first snack. Linda went into the kitchen and came back with an apple. Madonna had come halfway into the house, and she was hungrily watching Linda's hands. Linda dropped the apple in front of Madonna, who happily chomped it up.

Madonna still would not leave. She was sure there was more food. Linda slowly closed the door so as to push Madonna back onto the front porch. Linda could hear Madonna snuffling around the corners, looking for any extra food that might have fallen. Finally, the not-so-little piglet wandered off, thumping along the porch as she left.

Chapter Three
Disgruntled

A few weeks later, Linda heard
another snuffle and grunt. This time,
there was a much louder thud against
the door.

Linda opened the door to find an even
larger Madonna. She remembered

reading somewhere that a well-fed pig grew up very quickly. A few weeks before, Madonna had been a cute little piglet. Now she was beginning to look more like a barrel of potatoes with feet.

Linda gave Madonna a potato. Down it went. Then she went into the kitchen and came back with an apple.

By this time, Madonna had come through the doorway and was far inside the house. Linda gave her the apple, and down it went, too. Madonna took a few more steps inside and looked around— she wasn't going to leave. Linda went back into the kitchen and looked around for more food.

Madonna followed her and quickly found the cat food.

She slurped her way through both the cat food *and* the saucer of milk.

When Madonna was happy, she grunted loudly. Linda remembered where the word *disgruntled* came from—a pig that didn't *gruntle* was not a happy pig.

Linda realized she had to move quickly, before Madonna found more things to get into. While Madonna was still content from her few snacks, Linda bent down, placed a hand behind each of the pig's back legs, and gently pushed Madonna toward the door. Madonna slid and skidded across the polished tiles on the kitchen floor toward the door.

Finally, Linda managed to shove her visitor outside. Madonna had a last look around and wandered off.

Linda wiped the sweat from her brow, cleaned up the floor around the cat's food dishes, and returned to her studio. She looked at some of her early sketches of Madonna and realized that the piglet was now much, much bigger, and well on her way to being a huge pig. How big would she grow? How big does a pig get?

That weekend, Linda took a trip around the Bay of Islands to paint scenery. She was gone for a couple of weeks. When she came back, she wondered if Madonna would call again.

She didn't have long to wait.

Chapter Four
The Pig Tamer

There was the usual snuffle at the door. Linda opened the door, with the potato already in her hand, determined to keep the pig outside. In one swift movement Madonna plucked the potato from Linda's hand and galloped past her,

almost knocking her over. Madonna was much bigger than Linda thought she would be.

Madonna ran headlong toward the cat food dishes, running right over them. She snuffled up the cat's tuna fish and spilled the saucer of milk all over the floor. Her back feet spread the milk around in patterns like the ones in TV commercials before the magic floor cleaner comes to the rescue.

Linda could only stand and watch as Madonna gulped down everything in sight. Linda vowed never to tell her cat, or anyone else, that they "ate like pigs," now that she had seen a real pig in action.

While Linda was wondering what to do next, Madonna headed for the entrance to the hall and decided to go exploring. At each doorway in the hall, she would pause and poke her snout—still covered with tuna fish—into the room. When she decided there was no food in the room, she continued her steady stroll through the house.

Finally, she reached the end of the hall and ran into the bedroom.

"This is not good," thought Linda. Madonna looked as though she wanted to settle down for a snooze.

Linda remembered reading that some families used to bring pigs into their beds at night to share their warmth in winter. She thought that was fine for people who owned pigs, but the last thing she wanted was to wake up one morning and find Madonna in her bed.

Then Madonna poked her fishy snout into the closet, where she looked thoughtfully at some of the clothes.

Linda knew right then that she had to do something. She hurried back to the kitchen and opened a full box of dry cat food. She poured a small pile onto the floor in the middle of the hall.

Madonna snuffled her way out of the bedroom, ate the pile of cat food, and looked excitedly at the box in Linda's hand.

Linda picked up a dining-room chair and tried to shove Madonna on the rump to make her move back toward the kitchen. She felt just like a lion tamer in a circus.

Madonna gave Linda a look that made her decide to put down the chair and abandon her brief career as a pig tamer. Linda then tried to push Madonna down the hall, with both

hands on the pig's rump. It had worked before, but this time she may as well have tried to push a truck. Madonna had grown, and her feet dug into the carpet.

Linda realized that this was a case for brains, not brawn. She hoped that Madonna was not quite as smart as she looked.

This time Linda shook the box of dry cat food out onto the floor in a little trail for Madonna to follow. The trail led from Madonna's snout:

- down the hallway,
- through the kitchen,
- out the back door,
- down the steps,
- through the courtyard,
- and into the garden.

Madonna followed her, snuffling up

the cat food as she went. Linda thought it was like being followed by a large, black, hairy vacuum cleaner.

Once Madonna had snuffled her way out the front door and into the yard, Linda started running as she made the trail. Then she doubled back toward the house, ran inside, and closed the door. She watched Madonna's curly tail disappear down the garden path, still following the trail of cat food.

Eventually, Madonna wandered across the garden toward the opening in the back fence. On the way, she stopped to check out the compost pile. It was obviously full of smelly delights, which she found by tossing rotting vegetables and plants all over the yard.

Madonna's next stop was the row of seed trays full of seedlings. She must have heard that salad greens were healthy. She quickly ate and ran over the seedlings until they were gone. The mess was terrible.

At last she was gone.

Chapter Five

Twenty-Two Meals a Day!

Several weeks went by with no sign of Madonna.

One evening, Linda was walking along the valley road when she saw Mr. Forester repairing the front fence. She stopped to chat.

Before she could ask about Madonna, Mr. Forester pointed to the fence.

"This hole is Madonna's work," he said. "We made a pet of her when she was a piglet. But then she grew up—we never imagined how powerful a pig can be. And boy, could she eat!" He turned his eyes up to the sky.

"Yes, I know" said Linda.

"I suppose you do," said Mr. Forester. "From what I hear, half the families in the valley fell into the trap. No wonder she grew so fast—she must have been having twenty-two meals a day!

"We wondered what to do," he said. "We still remembered her as a pet piglet. I could never have sent her off to a regular pig farm. The kids would have known, no matter what I said."

"So, what did you do?" asked Linda.

"Well, we all thought she was a Captain Cook pig. You know, unusual, but nothing special. Then someone from way up the road took one look at her and told us she was a *Kune Kune* pig. I guess those are rare around here. He was real excited about it. He said he would love to breed her. So she's gone to live up there.

"We go over to see her sometimes. She remembers us—you can tell. But she's surrounded by four pig troughs and lots of other pigs, all growing up together. They treat the pigs just like pets up there. So she'll have a long and happy life. And now I can fix all these fences."

"I'm glad it's worked out well for everyone," said Linda. "Madonna was so charming when she was a piglet. I suppose we all forgot she would grow

up. She must have wondered why we all began to treat her so differently. She must have been confused."

Mr. Forester smiled and went back to fixing the fence.

Linda continued her walk. As she walked along the road, she remembered the young Madonna enjoying the same walk. Soon she was recalling some of the happiest times of her own childhood.

It was good to think back to those happy times. She wondered if Madonna sometimes thought about her own youth—when she visited everyone in the valley and had twenty-two meals a day.